Good Communications

Good Communications

– What every manager should need to know

JOHN HARGREAVES

A HALSTED PRESS BOOK

JOHN WILEY & SONS
New York – Toronto

*English language edition, except USA and Canada
published by*
Associated Business Programmes Ltd
17 Buckingham Gate, London SW1

Published in the USA and Canada by
Halsted Press, a Division of
John Wiley & Sons Inc
New York

First published 1977

Library of Congress Cataloging in Publication Data

Hargreaves, Basil John Alexander
  Good Communications

  "A Halsted Press Book"
  1. Communication in management.
I. Title.
HF5718.H287   1976   658.4'5   76-40317

ISBN 0-470-98958-0

**Printed in Great Britain by offset lithography by
Billing & Sons Ltd, Guildford, London and Worcester**

Contents

Part IV   **The techniques of communications**

Introduction

'Communications' has become a fashionable word. 'Good' communications – whatever they may be – are said to be the cure for industrial ills; 'bad' communications are looked on as their cause or scapegoat. 'Communications' is a term that can mean all things to all men. It can be used in the narrowest sense, for instance, to define a telephone procedure; or it can be used broadly to cover aspects of the activities of an entire organisation. Often it is not defined at all and remains in the realm, so convenient to Lewis Carroll's Humpty Dumpty, of words that can mean what we choose them to mean. It is a subject that is believed to be either obvious or esoteric. In the first case, it follows that anyone may consider himself to be an expert communicator. In the second, it becomes reasonable to assume that communications is a burden to be unloaded with a clear conscience upon a department of specialists, bearded, mysterious, but nevertheless experts in this work. Both assumptions are unwarrantable.

Communications are not necessarily obvious, though they are anything but esoteric. They are concerned with people. People deal with other people and, in so doing, they communicate with them. If they communicate well, they will be understood. If they do it badly, they will not and this will have bad effects. Any appreciable misunderstanding about what someone is required to know or do will produce an appreciable degree of inefficiency. Total misunderstanding will probably lead to total inefficiency because it in turn is likely to lead to work stoppages. There is thus a direct relationship between the effectiveness of communications and the efficiency of an organisation.

We are constantly establishing relationships with people – relationships which vary from one moment to the next. The success of our communications depends on the way in which we can guide and preserve these relationships; once an individual is angry or sullen, all attempts at communication break down. 'There are none so deaf as those who will not hear', and, at best, it is unwise to expect a rational response from our audience. One cannot explain something to someone who does not understand the concept. In a sense, communications can only bring out what is already there. Much of the art can be learned in our informal moments, away from the office, at home with our families. The trouble is that we do not carry the lessons learned there into the more formal atmosphere of business.

Yet it is in business of all places that the need to communicate is found. The corporation is the aggregate of its people. The nervous system of this body corporate consists of its lines of communication. It is these which can bring together the efforts of individuals and departments in pursuit of a given end, which can make the whole greater than the sum of its parts and which, if lacking, can deny cohesion to the enterprise. The allegiance and participation of one's employees cannot be gained, however, by the provision of an industrial welfare state. Man needs more than an appeal to his physical needs; the real message, which will inspire him to give of his best, must appeal to his mind. Good communication leads to intelligent participation and this, in turn, is the corner-stone for greater efficiency.

We live in a technological age, in which many routine and clerical processes are being replaced by automation, so that the human factor in business assumes greater importance than ever. We also live at a time when the established order is being challenged at every point, and its weaknesses and shortcomings are being exploited by those who do not necessarily serve the interests of those whom they profess to champion. At a time of higher education and greater independence of thought, people expect and need to know what is going on and why. The paternalism of management in the past must be exchanged for a willingness on the part of every manager to communicate intelligently and seek the co-operation of those with whom he works. In this, he can be aided by new approaches to the problem that will transform communications from being just an art into a science.

The state of industrial relations and efficiency in Britain today leads us to the conclusion that negotiating machinery, even when there is a will, is not alone sufficient to bring peace and productivity. A deeper, conscious man-manager relationship is needed if basic discords and misunderstandings are to be removed. The responsibility for this cannot be delegated: it is the job of every manager.

This book deliberately avoids the subject of negotiating procedures and, indeed, relations with trade unions as a whole. Likewise, it avoids discussion of various kinds of group training and self-analysis taught by eminent, if somewhat academic, institutions. Instead, it is confined to a discussion of communications as it applies to the line manager and sets out certain guiding principles to help him.

This book is in four main parts. First, there is an answer to the questions. 'Why bother to communicate?' and 'Why should it be me?' This throws reponsibility back on the line manager to whom this book is directed. The second part then examines the structure of communications and their flow downwards, upwards and sideways. The third section, inspired by Rudyard Kipling, though not to his knowledge, gives some checkpoints for successful communication, and the last deals briefly with some of the available techniques.

This simple approach to a deep subject has arisen from the author's own experience in training sessions with first and second line managers in a number of organisations. The approach is geared to the needs of practising managers who need to have a working and practical understanding of an essential facet of their task. The success of this approach is measured only in the degree that they leave the lecture room, or complete their reading of the book, and then put the guidelines into practice.

In preparing these guidelines, the author has followed the not uncommon practice of gathering other men's flowers. Of the many people to whom he has talked, Bob Cooper, Public Affairs Adviser to the Esso Petroleum Company, John Garnett, Director, and Colin Minton of the Industrial Society, splendid examples of communicators in theory and practice, must be singled out. To the members of the staff of the Industrial Society, I am most grateful. Much is owed to their thinking and example. Having made these acknowledgements, it remains to say that the views in this book are the author's own and do not imply endorsement either by the organisations which have helped him or the one by which he is employed.

In addition, there may be many who have written on this subject in the past who may recognise phrases or viewpoints that they have employed. If so, the failure to attribute to them is not deliberate but rather reflects the degree of success with which they have communicated – a degree that has caused their readers to embrace their wisdom as their own!

Finally, in these acknowledgements, is the one to my secretary, Rosemary Drew, whose patience extended to more than one version of this book.

PART I

The reasons for communication

1. Why communicate?

The importance of communications was recognised, though in a negative way, as early as 500 BC when a Greek historian noted that the slave labour forces in Egypt were guarded by soldiers who were unable to speak their language. This inability to communicate was a safeguard against the possibility of bribery and corruption and it is perhaps worth noting that, some 2500 years later, guards on the Berlin Wall were chosen for not dissimilar qualifications.

More seriously, and nearer home, the inability either to listen or to convey understanding to the recipients of a message can be seen to lie at the root of many of our industrial problems. An example of this came in a television programme reporting on a strike that was taking place in a factory. The interviewer talked to one of the men picketing the gates and asked him why he was supporting the strike. Understandably, in such a situation, the man at first had some difficulty in expressing himself but the one comment he eventually made was, 'Well, management don't tell us what is going on.'

In this case, it would be wrong to suppose that poor communication was, in fact, the sole or even the major reason for the strike though it is significant that the man should have chosen to express his grievances in those

3

terms. On the other hand, the incident does illustrate the demoralising effect on those people who do not know what is going on in their organisations as well as the fact that those who do feel this way tend to draw pessimistic conclusions.

More will be said later about the potency of silence as a communicator but, as a general statement, it is not true that 'no news is good news'. The company chairman who announced that there would be redundancies, but that the number was not yet specified, invited resistance as well as displaying his lack of forward planning. The announcement of a move of location, without simultaneously indicating who might be affected, likewise destined the move to start on the wrong foot. A garage chain was to be taken over. Rumours of redundancies were rife. Five days before the takeover the garage hands were told that they would be interviewed the next day and a decision would then be made about whether they remained. As one remarked, 'We have no-one to represent us.' These are actual and recent examples, and it would not take long for any reader of our national newspapers to compile a volume of case histories of failure to inform people about matters affecting them.

Indeed, in today's industrial climate, the one way to ensure a following for those whose purpose in calling a strike in debateably the interests of their colleagues, is to provide an atmosphere of doubt and ignorance of 'what is going on'. There is a military axiom that the person who determines the flow of communications will dominate to a significant degree the commander's mind. The corollary is likewise true, namely, that the person who should determine this flow but fails to do so is ensuring that the gap will be filled by someone else.

And this is what is happening, with management increasingly on the defensive before communications that themselves are inaccurate and too often made by those whose legitimacy is questionable and whose role of communicator is by default.

The man on strike did not know what was going on but there are other lessons to be drawn from that incident if good communications are not to be seen merely in terms of employee morale or an activity to be indulged in: 'let's be kind to employees week'. The

"Let's be kind to employees" week

most important thing about the man on picket duty was not that his morale was low, even though that was undoubtedly the case, but that he was inefficient.

Doubtless the two were related but the fact remains that, certainly from a manager's point of view, there are few employees as inefficient as those who are not working at all.

There are, of course, degrees of inefficiency before the striking stage is reached. Labour turnover, absenteeism, unpunctuality, accidents, questionable performance and poor morale are all symptoms of the mental withdrawal of an individual from his work. Part of this will arise from the conditions of work itself in which man will reject what he feels debases him. This is a subject on its own. But another part inevitably comes when an individual loses his sense of purpose in his job. The extent to which this purpose is a factor of communication leads us into the study of the question, 'Why communicate?' and this question, in turn, can be subdivided into two more: 'Why bother?' and 'Why me?'

2. Why bother?

Why bother to communicate? To put things at their most clinical, efforts of business are directed to a single end, namely, getting the job done. To attain this objective, it is necessary to satisfy the needs of those who have a stake in the organisation – its employees, customers, shareholders and the community – and to make the optimum use of capital, material and human resources. The effect of meeting this objective will inevitably be that the morale of employees will be high, and that the organisation is likely to be socially useful, for it will have the capacity to be so. 'She was poor but she was honest,' may typify Victorian morality but in fact it is perfectly possible to be rich, honest and useful as well. In both the services and civilian life, the most efficient organisation has generally proved to be the one with the highest morale. Massive under-employment, from which Britain suffers more than most, and a lack of commitment to the job are conducive neither to efficiency nor to morale.

Are we efficient?

Recent figures issued by the Department of Employment show that, out of the 22 million employees in

7

employment in Great Britain, there are currently between 8 and 10 million job changes annually. These
figures can, in fact, mislead because the number of
people who change their job more than once a year
offsets the total, static population which is probably
greater. Nevertheless, of these changes, only 10 per
cent were made to an expanding job.

In addition to these figures of change:

(a) for the year ending June 1972 (the most recent
     figures at the time of writing) 306 million man
     days were lost through certified sickness and
     other absenteeism doubles this.

(b) In the same period, 18.3 million man days were
     lost through accidents (cp. 16.6 million in the
     previous year).

(c) In 1974, 14.7 million days were lost through
     strikes (cp. 7.2 million for the previous year).

The number of strikes has increased dramatically for
several reasons. Unemployment figures have soared
for primarily recession reasons, though the shakeout of
over-manned areas is by no means complete. But,
whatever the present extenuating circumstances, the
question that can be reasonably asked is how much was
low morale the cause of these changes and lost days,
either because there was poor motivation, or because
those who do not know 'what is going on', and mistrust
their management, fall ready prey to those who wish to
exploit grievances?

In looking at the chronic over-manning and under-
employment in British industry, how much of the
entrenched attitudes stem from fear, which itself is the

by-product of ignorance and doubt? And, if so, has communication failed to reduce that level of apprehension?

Co-operation in safety standards is not imposed. In a free society, it comes from beneath. But the reason for it and the will to co-operate must be communicated and has that always taken place?

A strike leader in a key industry was reminded of the public concern that was felt because of the disastrous effect strike action would have on the country. His reply was that the public might well be concerned because it had been living off the backs of these workers for long enough. He was not a militant so much as a man who was still in the power of the past. Why had no new perspectives and ideas been communicated?

Whatever the immediate answer to these questions, the degree to which we make the best use of labour resources in this country is, at least, questionable. Moreover, whatever the cause, the disruptive effect of these changes and absences in the organisations where they occur can be imagined. We all know the effect of someone being away from our own department.

An important part in remedying this situation, even though it has, through neglect and other causes, reached its present unhappy level, must be played by effective communications and the purpose of this book is to explore how this may be.

Where is the motivation?

Time and money spent on motivation, that is getting people to give of their best, is well justified. Moreover, there is a world of difference between getting people to give of their best and merely seeking to get the most out of them. The latter can build up resentment; the former depends on intelligent co-operation.

It has been said that, left to themselves, people will work at between 40 – 50 per cent of their efficiency. If incentives are introduced, this level can rise to some 70 per cent. To raise it further another factor is required to motivate them. What is it?

Man requires more than the satisfaction of his economic needs to bring out the best in him. Indeed, there is overwhelming evidence to show that, once these basic economic needs are satisfied, the priorities in an individual's life change and his extra efforts will be directed to other than merely material ends: to things that enhance the quality of his life.

In any organisation, be it social, religious or industrial, an individual has a need for three things. He must feel that he belongs, he requires an outlet for self-expression and he must have a purpose. In a world of accelerating change, the means of achieving these needs are under review because their former basis is disappearing.

In an earlier, agricultural society, the sense of belonging was not difficult to feel. However poor they were, people had a recognised role. They had their station in life, a sense of security; basic needs were, on the whole, supplied under the old squirarchy and an identity was felt with a larger family. This 'order' was underlined by religious teaching and, whatever the abuses of the system, there was a stability that has yet to be re-captured.

The growing urbanisation of the country brought with it a challenge to all this. The social and religious continuum on which it was based was questioned and even the attempt to continue the system within an industrial society through, what pejoratively now, is called paternalism, was not enough.

The need for self-expression has likewise to find new outlets within a society which appears to conspire against individual expression. Mass techniques, mass production and mass communications appear to leave few channels for such expression, and the urge merely to be different is a poor substitute. In a more educated society an individual wants to feel he is expressing all his capabilities – physical and mental – if the job that he does is to be seen, in his eyes, to be worth doing with all his capacity.

This leads to his third requirement, the need for a purpose. 'To dig a ditch to earn enough money to keep alive to dig a ditch', is clearly an inadequate purpose. Nor is it enough to pass down objectives through a hierarchic management structure. The hierarchy, or pyramid, structure of command served the Roman Legions where one man communicated with ten, ten with a hundred and so on. It is not enough for people who think and question. Increasingly today it is situations, not people, that dominate, and the good manager is the one who can interpret the demands of a situation so that all who are concerned in responding to it feel that they are working, under the situation, but *with* people. In this, the degree to which an individual feels informed relates directly to his efficiency.

The exchange of the old order for an industrial society where the pay packet is not enough to satisfy man's needs has brought with it, as the new conditions have begun to be felt, a lack of motivation. How many strikes, ostensibly for money, are really directed against the conditions and structures of the place of work? Money is the tangible objective; it is easy to articulate a demand but it is by no means the real reason for industrial action.

Be this as it may, management today has to supply the motivating force that will cause people to give of their best. It has to communicate an understanding of the individual's role and importance in the company, to instil a purpose and provide the means whereby someone can feel he is expressing all of his or her capabilities. During a Royal visit to the Mayo Clinic in the United States, the kitchens were visited and a coloured worker who was washing up explained the all-importance of his job. 'You see', he said, 'if I do not do this job properly, those specialists upstairs will get germs and won't be able to do theirs.' Simple? Possibly, but someone had certainly conveyed to him a purpose for his work. How do we, as managers, help those who work with us to feel, so to speak, that when they come to work on Monday morning, they do so with an attitude that encourages good as opposed to indifferent standards.

It is because motivation has to be communicated that we *bother*. Communication is directed to efficiency, not merely to the attainment of good human relations even though the latter will follow. The manager who was on such good terms with his people that he 'knew all about an impending strike an hour before it happened', may have achieved human relations of a sort but they did not lead to efficiency. Communicating purpose and understanding is a daily, an hourly task. The concern engendered by a crisis situation is no substitute for the constant fostering of good relations within which the matters that can lead to crisis may be resolved. In motor car terms, we are talking about preventive maintenance rather than the provision of a breakdown service. Both are necessary but the first can help obviate the need for the second and prevention is preferable to cure.

So, why bother? Because good motivation, well communicated, builds efficiency. It instils pride, purpose and understanding in work. It lays the foundation for people to work together under the demands of situations. It invites the intelligent use of *all* the human resources in the enterprise and recognises that the prime asset in any organisation is the good-will of the people it is dealing with, both inside and out.

3. Why me?

The second subsidiary question that was posed was 'Why me?' The point in answering it is to show that communicating with his people is part of the job of the manager and something on which he should be measured in the same way that he is measured and rewarded for his ability to look after his budgets, develop his people and perform his functional task.

It is only comparatively recently that management in this country has begun to take an interest in communications as a technique, and thus recognise that the relaying of information, ideas and attitudes between individuals and groups in an organisation is an essential part of management responsibility, and one that has had too little attention paid to it.

And here is the answer to the second question, 'Why me?' It is a popular misconception that all that is required to ensure good communications is a battery of formal techniques such as house journals, notice boards, instruction letters and the like. In fact, the medium is not the message in most cases and the factory manager who attached a three hundred page book of regulations and procedures to the notice board did not apparently realise he was not communicating! The conveyance of understanding between two or more

15

A battery of formal techniques.

people is not assured by the vehicle that conveys it.

It must be a fundamental principle that the responsibility for good communications lies fairly and squarely with line management at all levels even though, as with personnel and finance, guidelines may be set by a professional, directing staff. Consultants, particularly in the United States, are suggesting that managers may have to spend as much as 80 per cent of their time communicating. Certainly it is a major part of any manager's responsibility. Formal techniques can do no more than supplement these line channels and there is an abundance of evidence to show how unrealistic it is to assume that, on their own, they can do much to influence employees' attitudes or impart information.

Nor should they. Personal face-to-face communication must always be by far the most effective way to exchange information and convey understanding. Communicating well is a management skill, though not separate from its other skills. It is one of the several factors that are built into every single management action and decision. The ability to communicate – to make himself understood in the right way at the right time – is part of a manager's job. It is no more, but equally no less, important than other specifications for a good manager. It is a skill, however, that for too long has escaped general recognition; it is deliberate rather than *ad hoc*, practice. Yet how vital to the efficiency and well-being of any group of people that they work in a climate of understanding and how disastrous if they do not!

To communicate successfully implies knowing the people with whom one is communicating and knowing the changing climate in which a communication takes place. Personal problems, work frustrations, health, relationships can all affect this climate. Who, but the manager, can expect to know this climate well? The degree of sensitivity that is imposed on managers in really knowing their people is considerable. Here the organisation of the Roman Legion had its uses, and it may not be coincidence that sections in the Services and teams in sports still tend to maintain a ratio of one leader to ten. On the other hand, the average ratio of managers in British factories would make it difficult to maintain this close personal awareness of all that makes someone 'tick'.

Sensitivity, interest, warmth and understanding are not conveyed by media but are intensely personal qualities that do or do not exist in people. When they are present they inspire. When they are not, there is no substitute in techniques. Reliance on formal techniques or specialists to achieve this can only lead to the neglect of a line manager's own responsibility.

Napoleon's adage that there are not bad soldiers, only bad officers, is true in business. The great difference between communicating with a person, as opposed to a machine, is that the person's acceptance is governed by both facts and emotion. It would be wrong to assume that people always react rationally, but a machine responds only to facts. A person says 'prove it'. To convey an understanding that causes communication to be accepted requires skill and sensitivity. A person may react in one of two ways. He may say, 'I find it difficult to understand but I have confidence in you, so I am prepared to accept what you say,' or he may say, 'I am sure all you say is right but I don't like your face so am not prepared to accept it.' At the lower levels of supervision, this is particularly so, and there is a widespread lack of skill in communicating face to face.

The ingredient of trust is built up over time, but can be lost in a minute. It stems from the manager's daily demeanour, from the hundred small acts and gestures that either bring out or stifle the best in people. Managers must lead, however unpalatable that word is at present. Despite the current drive for equality, it remains true that:

> When everyone is somebody
> Then no one's anybody.

In no way does this deny respect for every individual but it does put an onus on management to lead by the standards it sets. The manager must not only be able to communicate professionally but he must also help create the climate in which the communication can take place. Management determines the quality of a firm's industrial relations as well as the standard of its efficiency.

The answer to the manager's question, 'What, then, do we pay a professional department for?' is, crudely, 'Not to do your work for you!'

Summary

This opening section is not intended to offer either a social history of Britain or an essay on the qualities of leadership. Its purpose is simply to give a degree of background in the course of answering the questions, 'Why bother to communicate?' and 'Why should management do it?' It also provides historical perspective for those in industry who wish to introduce one or more sessions on communications in their management training courses. There are still too many organisations where this introduction has to be made.

A useful exercise to test the effectiveness of these lines of communication is to take a number of recent top management decisions or notices and trace the method of passing and the degree of retention down the line. Then the way in which queries have been satisfied can also be traced.

One of the more general and predictable patterns in this kind of survey is that the biggest group to feel left out of the chain of communications are the first line managers, supervisors and foremen. It is rare for some whole group not to be left out of the information process, and rarer still for the degree of awareness to be consistent.

Given the background of this section and the recognition that communication is part of line management proficiency, it is then possible to examine the methods by which communication can take place. This is something which can be taught together with a knowledge of the techniques that can be used, and these are the subjects of the following sections.

PART II

The structure of communications

Foreword

The purpose of communications is to convey understanding. Understanding is more than words and more than techniques. It is also more than the organisation that is set up to allow the passage of communication. Nevertheless, the organisational structure must exist. Communications flow downward, upward and laterally. These are the bare bones of communication into which the warmth and spirit of the communicator breathes life. But, without the formal structure, too many mistakes of ommission and commission can occur.

The organisation must include top management involvement and sympathy. The person responsible for communications must report to the top. Without this recognition of their importance, communications are doomed to be second best for they will take place in spite of, instead of because of, the key decision makers.

To the formal *means* for communication and the *recognition* of their importance, the social skills of a manager can be added. These will determine the *quality* of the communication. These three ingredients, together with management training, in communication, at least, set the scene for an objective which the Industrial Society defines as 'Communicating an understanding of those

matters, which cause an individual to give of his best to his
work'.

4. Downward communications

The subject of downward communication is treated in more detail in the third section of this book. At this stage, however, there is a need to stress that a formal method must exist for communicating down the line. If it does not, the risk is that whole groups of people may be left out, particularly when the decision to communicate is made in a hurry. The method includes both the sequence in which the communication itself is delivered and the method by which it is passed.

The sequence is important because it allows the whole message to be passed in a series of distinct, logical and progressive steps. In the case of instructions, the reason for the communication must first be stated. What is the objective? What is it that one hopes to achieve? This may then be elaborated by describing some of the circumstances that are relevant before going on to define the way in which the stated purpose will be achieved. The communication is not complete until an opportunity has been given to test whether the message has been received.

The chain of communication

The lines of communication, however, are essential if even the best prepared message is to succeed and in industry these formal lines are sadly lacking. In this matter, there is much to be learned from the Services. The Army, for example, has been practising communications for 250 years because its morale and performance have depended largely on them. Other groups, not dissimilar to the structure of the Legions, have allowed information to be passed down the line, in a recognised sequence and through a formal chain of command, so that each individual has been assured of the knowledge that he requires to do his particular job and to understand how it relates to those around him.

There is no less a need in industry for a formal, systematic drill for communicating with people; a drill that must involve each manager and his people and a drill that implies regular, planned meetings. Unless communications are structured in this way, messages go by default and people get left out of the communication process.

There are a number of guidelines. First, the meetings must be regular and this in itself will make organisational demands on managers, since to call together people in a group and take account of shifts and people away on assignments will mean effort and determination if the meeting is to take place. The priority attached to communications will determine whether, in fact, people who work away from their head office do come in for regular meetings and feel it important to their job that they do so.

In industrial, as opposed to Service life, this structured approach to communicating has been pioneered and promulgated by the Industrial Society. Prefaced by the sage comment that 'people cannot possibly partici- pate in decisions until they *understand* what is going on', a series of publications offer mangement guidance in forming and running 'briefing groups'. How to com- municate the 'four P's' (see below) and examples of the effectiveness of this approach appear, in particular, in the Society's publications: Briefing Groups: An intro- duction and operational manual and A Pocket Guide to Briefing Groups.

The meetings must be manageable and there must be a common denominator of interest. A manageable group for a successful, two-way discussion is unlikely to number more than ten to fifteen people. The common interest may be departmental or professional and it will provide the purpose for the meeting.

Meetings of this kind must be held by the manager of the group. They are meetings to pass understanding and weld together people in a team. This is unlike mere instruction which can reasonably be left to third parties. In these meetings, managers are performing part of their own management task. Of course, the communi- cation chain must start at the top and the process then ensures that no level in the organisation, from top to bottom, is left out. The language in which the message may be passed will vary: the purpose of communicating understanding will not.

Four subjects for consideration at such meetings are given in a paper by the Director of the Industrial Socie- ty, John Garnett.* They are classified as the 'four P's', standing for 'progress', 'people', 'policy' and 'points': progress reports, news of what is happening to people,

---

* Management's Responsibility for Effective Communication, Fifth STC Communication Lecture, 1975.

policies that affect people, and points of interest or relevance to the job, all communicate an understanding that helps people to give of their best.

A final reminder on the working of this chain of communication. A record must be kept and, as the links in the chain increase in number, the spoken message must be supplemented with a written brief to prevent distortion.

Induction

One area, in particular, where planned communication is needed is the induction of new employees. It is all too easy for individuals or groups to find that they have been a long time in the firm before receiving any formal induction. It is quite common for them never to receive it.

Induction can be carried out at two levels. The manager can and must take time when an employee joins his department to explain what the department does, who the key people are, who the employee can turn to to ask questions and some basic policies and practices in the firm. Without this basic instruction, a new arrival is not equipped for work. It is also helpful to appoint someone in the group to show the new employee around.

More formal induction into the firm's products, organisation, general practices and so on will best be carried out by the personnel department and it can be arranged in groups. The standard of presentation must be high, ample opportunity must be given to ask questions and the atmosphere must not be overwhelming!

Induction is a formal communication. It must be planned and enforced. Allowing an employee to 'pick things up and he goes along' is not a substitute even though, apparently, it is often thought to be.

Downward communication does not just happen. Messages of a sort will always be passed but, if they are to be accurate and helpful, the routes by which they pass must be prepared. Failure to supply these routes will result in misrepresentation, misconception and even resistance. Time and trouble spent on assuring them will, as ample evidence already shows, result in greater efficiency, a greater commitment to the job, a finer degree of mutual understanding and a happier atmosphere at work.

Management resolve to communicate the truth to its people and to ensure that they are 'in the know', combined with a knowledge on the part of employees that they will be told the truth and be kept in the picture, will be the only key to opening the door on a new and improved phase of industrial relations. Without it, no legislation can by itself bring this state about.

Measuring the effectiveness of downward communications groups is not entirely straightforward. It takes time to assess results and there is an inevitable interplay of other factors. As one plant manager put it, 'the direct costs of holding these meetings in office hours is £30,000, but we have never lost £30,000 worth of production!'

On the other hand the absentee rate in another plant was reduced from 40 per cent to 14 per cent in eighteen months after there had been a structured campaign to communicate to employees just what the effect of absenteeism was. In a different plant, manufacturing cigarettes, the absentee rate dropped from 30 per cent to 15 per cent following the introduction of briefing groups.

In yet another factory, briefing groups were introduced at the time of the introduction of a new technology to which there had been an initial adverse reaction. Strikes had been threatened and the decision to brief employees systematically was only taken after that. In fact, the briefing was successful, and the employees' reaction then was, 'If you had told us in the first place, it would have been all right!'

How often, at times of industrial unrest, could this be said? There are countless examples of discussions going sour when there is failure to communicate; countless more of talks going smoothly, strikes averted and productivity increased when people know what is going on.

5. Upward communications

The free flow of communication must go upward as well as downward. The measurement of the effect of a downward message, though necessary, does not constitute an upward flow. There are a number of evident reasons why this flow is important as part of the arterial system of the body corporate.

The first is that, without the antennae that can sense the attitudes and opinions of those with whom the company has to deal, management is deprived of an area of knowledge that is essential to its planning. This kind of knowledge is as important as knowledge relating, for example, to market conditions – a part of the total environment within which the company operates.

Though the prime interest of the manager will be with those who report to him he must, as part of his company's management team, recognise that his sensitivity to other groups of people with whom he is in contact, such as vendors, customers and the community may be of great importance also.

A second reason for encouraging upward communications is that it avoids waste. Apart from any other consideration, it is sheer inefficiency not to tap the immense store of useful experience and imagination that exists throughout any organisation. The contribution

may be in 'physical' terms, such as technical contribu-
tions, organisational amendments or ideas relating to the
physical environment. It may also be in the form of ideas
relating to the future of the firm, the climate in which it
operates and the messages, as opposed to just the
products, that it purveys.

Third, there is the question of motivation and this
applies particularly to the larger organisations. It is that
an employee must be made to feel that the company is
interested in, anxious to benefit from and prepared to
reward the *whole* of an individual's capabilities and not
just the work that he can do with his hands. His morale,
desire to co-operate and so his efficiency will certainly
be impaired if he feels that his ideas and opinions are
being ignored or dismissed.

A free upwards flow of communication is only
encouraged, however, if managers are prepared to
listen and not regard what they hear as interference in
their job or merely 'answering back'. In turn, this willingness to accept what comes through this upwards
flow will stem from a deep respect for every individual,
no matter what his position in the organisation.

Managers must want to be aware! An experiment
carried out in a large American corporation was reveal-
ing. A team of independent researchers deliberately
sowed rumours which, though harmless in themselves,
were sufficiently startling for them to be transmitted
readily from one point to another. The researchers
measured the speed and the levels to which the
rumours went. True to form, the grapevine carried the
rumours quickly downwards and sideways. Upwards,
they travelled at speed until they got near, but not into,
the executive offices. A 'ditch' outside the directors'
doors insulated them from such penetration! This is an

exercise that can be usefully repeated in other organisa- tions. The following illustrate some techniques for upward communications.

Suggestion schemes

One company of 15,000 employees has consistently shown a profit of over £20,000 per annum from its suggestion schemes, allowing for the full cost of administering it and rewarding those whose suggestions are adopted on a percentage of value to the company. This is by no means unique.

Ways can be sought also for inviting 'mental' suggestions or for indulging in what one organisation lugubriously called 'Operation Witpick'. Whatever class of suggestions are to be encouraged, it must be seen throughout the organisation to be worthwhile. Suggestions must be rewarded properly and the efforts of successful employees published.

Opinion surveys

Opinion surveys are a form of personnel audit in which employees are invited to state their opinions on a wide and intimate variety of subjects concerning themselves and their organisation. They must be carried out with complete anonymity so that no individual answer can be identified. An outside survey team can ensure this. The answers, in sufficient detail to be convincing, must be published and circulated to those who have taken part. Action must be seen to be taken where there are criticisms and the surveys must be repeated at intervals so that attitudes may be compared. It follows that, unless managers intend to do something about the answers, they are unwise to ask the questions.

Open door policies

In varying forms, all of which must be clearly understood, there are policies which allow any employee who feels that a grievance or concern has not be satisfied by his immediate manager, to go up the line – if necessary to the very top – until satisfaction can be obtained. In fact, good management at the lower levels should obviate the need for many of these cases. In practice, it may often be the cranks and professional grievance seekers who make use of it. But it is a safety valve and for that reason alone is valuable. It also puts the onus of good management onto the manager himself.

Speak up

One company refers to a 'speak up' programme. Any employee, including managers, can put in writing any question, comment or complaint and be guaranteed a full reply from the senior manager best qualified to deal with it. It is completely anonymous. Only, the writer and one staff co-ordinator ever know the individual's identity. The writer may request a personal answer or a written reply. Far from undermining line management, this programme has proved to be a useful way of dealing with matters that may reasonably be beyond an individual manager's competence to answer. Top management can explain its policies and thinking;

anomalies can be adjusted and there appears to be confidence in this technique.

Consultative committees

Because this book is aimed at the line manager and the day-to-day situations with which he must cope, the ommission of more structured negotiating procedures has been deliberate. The role of, and relationship with, union representatives have their own library.

Nevertheless, it is important for all managers to recognise that there are certain matters which have a collective, as opposed to an individual, interest and so there has to be a way of dealing with them. Systems and lines of communication that have been designed to deal with individual problems will not necessarily be adequate to cope with collective needs. Additional structures and techniques may be required, not to by-pass or replace line management responsibility, but to address the additional need.

There are techniques and channels of communication for consultation and also for negotiation and the expression of grievances. They differ from each other and are both totally separate from the process of management planning and control. It is the channel for consultation that is the concern of this section.

There is a deepening interest in all forms of participation and consultation. This is not merely because a better educated workforce wants to know why certain policies and decisions are made, but also because, as organisations get bigger and more dispersed and as technology makes conditions more complex, people need to know why. At times when economic conditions threaten jobs, the educated interest in what is going on is enhanced by a natural concern for their effect on individual lives. In one form or another, the move towards greater participation is going to gather, rather than lose, momentum.

Though the form and subject matter for discussion will vary, the purpose of any consultative mechanism is to enable facts and opinion to be available at the appropriate point in the organisation. If this can be done, then the result should be, first, a sense of involvement in an organisation that goes beyond any specific job and, second, a sense of participation in decision-making at all levels. Both effects are important as the balance between the organisation and worker changes, and efforts are made to move through understanding, rather than coercion.

What should be discussed?

There is a difference between what is and what should be discussed. In practice – and there is no one formula either across firms or across the country, though there is consistency of evidence to prove that Britain has much to unlearn – discussion often tends to range around sickness and health, amenities and other money spending activities. To confine deliberations to such subjects is insufficient.

If a consultative process is to be used properly its concerns should include matters affecting the immediate working environment, representation as something separate from unions and the opportunity to influence both shop floor participation and key decisions in the organisation. Subject matter inevitably will expand.

A Bow Group publication * suggests that the following are included as items for discussion:

(a) All matters of general economic interest to employees.

(b) Rules concerning recruitment, promotion, dismissal, training, safety, hours, holidays etc.

(c) Job evaluation, wage rates, closures, transfers, organisational changes.

It is perhaps worth making four comments at this stage, however, about consultative committees in general. The first is to remark that, unless the meetings are structured, prepared and built round a proper agenda, discussion will, indeed, tend to wander rather than lead to definitive conclusions and recommendations for action. The second is the observation that a consultative committee is there to consult! It is not unusual for management, having formed a committee, to be surprised that its members have opinions and are articulate in expressing them. Equally, it is true that such committees need to be used responsibly by their members and not misused by trouble makers. The third is that genuine consultation precedes rather than follows decision-making. Ideally, it is the proposal and not its implementation that should be discussed. Obviously, if the issue is sufficiently important it may become the subject of negotiation at a later stage, even though it started life in a consultative committee. The fourth is that meetings should be regular to avoid any associa-

* *Employee Participation*, Bow Group Report, 1973.

tion of such committees with 'bad news' meetings.

Who discusses?

The constitution of these committees has to allow for the involvement of those who direct the business, those who implement its policies and the employees on the shop floor. There are already vehicles for the expression of grievances and negotiation of wages. More is required for those who want a deeper involvement even though, necessarily, these may be a minority within the population.

Those on the committee must know that they can influence management decisions. An advisory or consultative committee advises or consults but a wise management listens. A correctly composed consultative committee which is used by management will indicate whether the concept of management in a particular organisation is one of conveying orders, or harnessing the combined abilities of managers and subordinates in a common endeavour to understand the demands of any situation and meet them, intelligently, together. In fact, the latter is the only realistic alternative. Problems begin with persuasion just as problem-solving begins with discussion. Management cannot impose safety precautions and avoidance of pollution, for example. People must be imbued with the desire to co-operate intelligently in these matters. So a body is needed to do this.

The consultative committee is a vehicle for responsible two-way communication. It can help push the level at which decisions are made down, not up. It can clarify the dividing line between consultation and negotiation. It can promote an understanding of corporate objectives and an involvement in their achievement. It can be a mechanism to tap ideas and to point out areas for change or emphasis better than can management alone. It can help management anticipate, rather than just respond to, changes in the law. As its name implies, however, it is a vehicle whereby people consult and listen to each other and not a vehicle for bludgeoning.

In short, managers communicate down about the task they want done. Representatives communicate up about the aspirations they feel.

Managers do not have to wait to be involved in consultative machinery. Here and now they can practice running their own pump. Instead of bringing in people one at a time, they can plan discussion situations.

The sequence of events, then, for the manager is 'Consult; Decide; Brief' – in that order!

6. Lateral communications

The last of our structural headings is the sideways flow of communication. The exchange of information between groups and individuals becomes harder as the organisation becomes larger or as the matters with which it deals become more technical.

As the firm grows, it is far simpler for people to continue to work in their own compartments. Amoeba-like, departments and functions sub-divide; the demarcation lines between them are not always clear and still less generally known; they may be physically separated between different buildings and the pressure of work will help people to forget who else is in their firm.

The compartmenting of daily life is also related to the complexity of the product. If it is a high technology firm, the temptation to remain within a discipline or to live a laboratory as opposed to a manufacturing or marketing life is great. One research firm in the United States has calculated that, if a project costs less than $100,000, it is cheaper to do it than to see if it has to be done.

One way of becoming communications-conscious in a large organisation is to appoint a communications representative at every regular or major meeting, with the job of thinking in terms of who can profitably learn from the proceedings of the meeting. Another simple, but often forgotten, aid to lateral communications is to forget the internal telephone and go and see the person instead! It is one of the most fruitful ways of helping managers to leave the highly specialised areas where they have probably been nurtured and to learn the broader outlook that they will require as they move to more senior positions. It is also the way in which they will come to appreciate that 'they' in other departments are actually human beings with hopes, worries and uncertainties like one's own, and who will be far more useful if treated as colleagues instead of opponents. It was a government department in the last war that put round the forlorn memorandum which read, 'Remember the man in the next department is not necessarily an enemy!'

Certain aids to technical communication are available. One, which can involve computers but whose principle can be adapted, is known as KWIC (Key Word in Context) indexing. It allows engineers and specialists throughout a wide-spread organisation to state certain key words which describe a particular interest area and to be on a mailing list for any publications or other information that relates to it. A computer search automatically supplies a list with a brief summary of the subject and, if further information is then required, a full text can be supplied. While it is not assumed that the units of all business organisations are yet computer-linked, it is nevertheless useful to recognise the type and direction of the new technology that is becoming available.

The last remark on lateral communications is that any communication must have a purpose. This apparently obvious remark is included to counter the suggestion made in one firm known to the author that, once one of its units had reached a critical mass of around 800 people, it was possible for the people in it to keep themselves fully occupied by writing memoranda to each other and calling meetings without actually engaging in any productive work!

Note: For further stimulus on the subject of lateral communications, the Rank audio-visual production *The GOYA effect* is recommended.

PART III

The servants of communications

Foreword

In this section we examine some of the elements that go into communications. These elements can be taught and the approach in this section is designed to offer material for those who do the teaching, as well as a system for those who are learning the subject to remember and practice. It is important to remember that this is a subject for classroom instruction. Even 'born communicators', if there really be such people, need their instinctive abilities harnessed to methods that have been tried.

Consciously, or not, Rudyard Kipling gave the clue to good communications in his poem;

> I keep six honest serving men
> (They taught me all I knew)
> Their names were WHAT and WHY and WHEN
> And HOW and WHERE and WHO.

These six interrogatory pronouns give us the key. We shall not go wrong if, every time we make a decision, become aware of some policy or take action affecting others, we ask ourselves, '*What* shall I say? *Why* do others need to know? *When* shall I say it? *How* shall I go about it? *Where* shall I do the telling? *Who* should be told?'

We now look at the answers to these questions.

7. The 'what' of communications

What we communicate means both 'what do I need to say?' and 'what do they need to know?' They are not necessarily the same. Its difference is that what others need to know may invite the minimum information whereas what I need to say should normally call forth the maximum. It is the difference between a manager benevolently keeping his staff in the picture and the recognition of their right to knowledge.

So this review of what we communicate starts, as does all communication, with the atmosphere in which we carry out the rules. What we have to communicate is information within a climate of understanding. The second determines the comprehension of the first.

This is why it is often wise to tell the maximum and there are three particular reasons for this. The first is that, although there may on occasions be some risk to security, the respect that is thus shown to the intelligence and status of employees more than offsets the risk that the more that is said, the more there is to be garbled. If someone is determined to breach security he is likely to get the information anyhow. On the other hand, in most cases respect engenders respect.

The second reason ties closely with the first. The grapevine will convey in an amazing way more than we

51

like to think. Moreover, the grapevine, even though it tends to be disconcertingly accurate, is nearly always uncharitable to those who make the decisions and therefore militates against the success of normal communication channels.

The third reason for generosity in communicating is that we build up capital. If the general rule is to tell as much as possible, then people will more willingly understand and accept those occasions when only the minimum can be said. Understanding is a two-way communication and, in nurturing it, we create the climate in which communication is made. For these three reasons, then, at least, the tendency to be secretive is both unnecessary on many occasions and harmful.

So much for the climate. What about the information itself that is to be imparted? A study by Princeton University of some major firms in the United States listed three types of information as being of most use to employees: that which gave them a better insight into their work and its relation to the work of others in the firm; that which gave them a sense of belonging; and that which improved their sense of status and importance in the organisation.

These are general points, but whatever else the individual may want to know, his main interest will be in matters that affect him personally or that he *believes* may do so. When told of plans for development, or the stream-lining of operations, he is less likely to say 'What a fine, progressive firm I work for,' than 'What will happen to me?'

Involvement starts at the level of the job, how it relates to others, how it is rewarded, what factors whether internal or external can affect it, and what its dependencies are. It then extends to matters that are

What about me?

tied to the success of the firm as a whole, and the community of which it is part. As responsibilities increase, so, too, will the need for an understanding of citizenship and economic literacy.

When an individual feels involved at each level, he is likely to give of his best. To communicate that which effectively helps him to do his job is the task of management. This information may be technical, personal or relating to policies, but each type can help the employee to know where he is going and how he relates to others.

One area of information that is worth singling out is that which relates to an individual's personal performance and standing in the firm. The practice of counsel and appraisal which, in varying forms, is gaining acceptance in British industry, allows a regular opportunity for someone to discuss formally with his manager his standing and prospects. These formal interviews, which of course do not obviate the need for regular interim communication, have to be prepared for by both sides. They have to relate to agreed objectives and the success of these interviews depends both on the honesty of the manager in saying exactly what he thinks and on the employee having the opportunity both to put his point of view frankly and to see what has been said about him. In any case, where the appraisal is committed to record, it should not only be seen by the employee but should be validated by the next line up of management. In this way some view can be obtained of a particular manager's own ability to assess people, since the next line can compare his assessment with that of others, as well as safeguarding against any apparent unfairness.

Finally, in the 'what' of communications, let us remember that over-communication is also possible. This does not gainsay the earlier remarks about generosity in communicating: it does mean that, as so often in his life, the manager must tread with the wisdom of Solomon and the delicacy of Agag!

8. The 'why' of communications

Two factors have contributed to the need for effective communications in industry. The first is the growth in education in areas where, in the case of immigrants and other disadvantaged people, the gap between the literate and illiterate is widening. The second factor relates to the size of industrial organisations.

Education

The education factor works both ways. As people's critical faculties develop, they want to know what is going on. They will ask 'why' and they will need to be told. It is worth noting that, for the first time, we now have a generation that has never known the hierarchy of authority. For the most part they have not undergone National Service; the acceptance of authority at home, in the school and in daily life is no longer natural and, indeed, there is evidence that it is being consciously undermined in many cases.

All this adds up to the fact that the Centurion who was able to say 'Do this and he doeth it,' must now say 'I want you to do this *because* . . .'

The element of intelligent participation in the decisions of the firm, rather than a blind acceptance of order, is becoming increasingly important. The form in which this participation takes place is debatable and is less important than the recognition that, if it is not provided, and if management does not explain what is going on, the encouragement to ask 'why' will still be there – to find out, or to make trouble.

This last point does not require much elaboration. The debate about whether beds have Reds under them is, for the purpose of this book, less relevant than an examination of the beds we have made. What is abundantly true, however, is that vacuums tend to be filled and if those whose task it is to explain 'why' do not do so, someone else will happily assume the responsibility.

At the other end of the scale is the need for special efforts in regard to the disadvantaged, themselves a ready prey for those who wish to disrupt. The industrial scene has been complicated both by the alarming numbers of illiterates or semi-literates emerging from our schooling system and by the growing number of immigrants whose basic need is often to learn the English language. How can these people give of their best and contribute to the efficiency of their organisations if the means of basic communication are lacking? Management takes time for courses and study. Do we give workers the same opportunity?

Size

The second factor which makes the emphasis on communications an imperative is that of size. A number of factors make communication harder as organisation become bigger.

The size of large corporations tends to destroy the atmosphere of the small firm. The individual finds it harder to know why particular decisions have been made and who has made them. Explanation and redress seem out of reach. There is a limit to the size of the unit to which an individual can relate. The smaller the group, the closer tends to be the relationship. Compare the difference between a small building firm where the members work together and often share risks with that which prevails on a large site.

From a communications point of view business organisations tend to be anything but the optimum size, so it is necessary to create opportunities in order to bring groups nearer to the ideal. This may mean establishing new entities within the existing organisations, increasing the ratio of managers and watching carefully the formal lines of communication. Of the latter, more will be said later.

Since organisations grow, sometimes haphazardly, the lines of communication get stretched: they become more complex and do not always follow a logical path. This extension has always been a formidable obstacle to the success either of armies or of management. There has to be a conscious effort to remember who may be involved in any particular project, as well as to have check points along the lines to see that information is getting through.

An effect of distance is, of course, speed. The flow of information can be slowed, particularly if it has to pass through the pending tray of several managers. Again, steps must be taken to watch and chase the flow, but the need for communicating becomes greater as the obstacles increase.

Finally, remoteness encourages belief in the mythical

race of 'they' as opposed to 'us', and the feeling of division between those who give and those who implement instructions is fostered. A leading employer averted a stoppage by getting junior managers and supervisors to brief people on management's side of the story so that employees undersood what decision had been taken and, more important, *why*.

On the whole too little study of these problems has been made. An analogy with the sea is appropriate. A sailing dinghy responds instantly to control and its turning circle is short, whereas the oil tanker, the Torrie Canyon, was unable to change course within the time between the anticipation and the experience of disaster. One giant corporation has been likened to a battleship towing a thousand skiers, half of whom get drowned every time it changes course!

The purpose of these notes is not to direct the reader's attention to the resolution of the problems of size but to warn him of the obstacles to communication that they present. More than ever, people in these circumstances will ask why, and managers must find a way to tell them. Otherwise the organisation and its people will suffer because, as Samuel Butler wrote:

> He who complies against his will
> Is of his own opinion still.

9. The 'when' of communications

'The "WHEN" of communications'

The illustration shows the embarrassing situation that can arise if the right information is conveyed to the right people at the wrong time. It also reminds us of the third of Kipling's serving men, 'when'. The decision to communicate must be accompanied by further decisions that relate to the timing of the message, and as many heartaches have been caused by failure in this direction as by any other mistakes in communication.

First comes the decision about how many people are to be told, and because they are likely to include people of differing seniority, attention must be given to the order in which they are told. A manager, for example, will need to know about something before his subordinates. Then the question arises of informing people outside as well as within the organisation. Employees can well think that they have a right to prior knowledge about their company and their reaction to reading some important news about it in the press before being informed by their management can vary from a mild 'wish that they had told me', to an exasperated 'how dare they not have told me'. The time of day or week is also important. There was a manager who had acquired a reputation for springing harsh decisions on his people. When he announced a meeting one Friday afternoon for the following Monday, it was understandable that many spent the weekend in unquiet speculation even though, on this occasion, the message was entirely innocent!

Four factors are particularly bound up with 'when'.

(*a*) *Speed*. Once a decision to communicate has been made it must be executed quickly. It is naïve to suppose that secrets can be kept and the experience of most industrialists is one of the uncanny prescience shown by employees concerning matters that had not, supposedly, been entertained by managers! The trouble with information that leaks the wrong way is that the grapevine will carry it and, since the grapevine is the fastest means of communication, beating it at any time is difficult. It is also the most dangerous because, apart from its generally uncharitable message, it hardens the attitude of those to whom the true message has to be given. There is nothing so impenetrable as the mind that is already made up.

In an employee opinion survey conducted by one company people were asked from which source they gained the most information about the company. This was distinct from another question which asked from which source they *expected* to gain this information, the answer to which was from management. To the first question, 12 per cent said that it came from their managers and 27 per cent from the grapevine, which meant that the managers were not regarded as the prevalent source for information. On the other hand, the positive effect of another company's communications was shown at the time of the Referendum when the management was regarded as the third most reliable source of information after television and BBC radio. Furthermore, when asked whether the company's information on the Common Market had made them more likely to vote one way or another, 32 per cent of the shop floor employees, 21 per cent clerical staff, 28 per cent managers and 43 per cent of the supervisers said it had. Of these the very large majority voted in favour of remaining in the EEC.

(*b*) *Synchronisation*. The employee's first awareness of news should be from his manager and not from outside the company. If the employee cannot be given the information first then there should be simultaneous internal and external releases. Managers should, where possible, inform supervisors and senior staff in advance so that they can be prepared for questions and so that management can speak with one voice. One point that is often overlooked concerns organisations with operations in more than one country. Not only must there be clear-cut embargoes on the publication of information before a certain date, but the actual time difference between, say, London and New York must be taken into account when synchronising a release.

(c) *Time*. Not only is the time of the day or week important but also the time in which communication takes place. If communicating is part of a manager's job, then he takes time to do it. Equally if communication is a two way business which will result in improved working performance, then it should normally take place in employee time. In one factory in the north-east of England, where output had not been too successful, a new manager decided that his priority was to communicate what was going on. He either did this regularly during working hours or, if absolutely necessary, he kept people behind and paid them at overtime rates for staying. At the end of one year, with no changes in product, staff or organisation, the output of that factory had risen by 20 per cent. No apparent factor had altered things except the insistence on communications, as the manager had recognised that communication was part of the job for everyone.

(d) *Repetition*. Public and individual ability to retain information is notoriously short. Therefore, in putting over important information, it generally will be necessary to repeat the message several times, using different media. It is well known that information which is conveyed both visably and orally is retained better than that which is conveyed by only one of these means.* Face-to-face communication can be reinforced by notice-boards, house journals and other formal techniques.

'When' has many pitfalls. Shutting the stable door after the horse has gone is not just an equestrian failing. Failing to prepare the ground so that the opportunity to communicate effectively is not wasted is another danger. As in the case of all the serving men, the communication of even good news takes thought and preparation but, to communicate something which people will be likely to resist, the work must be done consummately well.

---

* The accepted ratio is that hearing *and* seeing is ten times more effective than just hearing. *Doing* is one hundred times more effective than just hearing or seeing.

10.   The 'how' of communications

Language is a problem. Conversation at the simplest level can be misunderstood. Words mean different things to different people according to their individual experience and associations. People listen to what they believe is said, not to what is said. The barriers of class, history and education all come between people. What a wealth of different and emotional meaning can be attached, for example, to the word 'workers'. The power of the past is particularly strong and it is hard to escape its associations:

> The Devil was sick, the Devil a monk would be
> The Devil was well, the Devil a monk he'd be.

It is not enough that a manager understands a situation if he fails to convey this understanding to others. Understanding cannot be assumed. There was a notorious case of the Covent Garden porters and pitchers who complained that they could not understand the terms of agreement proposed by their employers. Certainly the terms were written in words not normally used by the readers, though it is probably true to say 'that, had they included an offer of an extra pound a week, they would have been understood even if they had been written in Swahili! But the opportunity for misconception had been given. Another illustration that comes to mind is the story of the strike that was called when management wished to go to arbitration. It turned out later that the men on the shop floor thought that the word 'arbitration' meant surrender.

Technicians tend to find it difficult to communicate without jargon. The *Daily Mirror* practices a rule that sentences have a maximum of seventeen words and that words with the minimum number of syllables are used. As for the man who says 'the answer is in the negative', well he is just a monument to pomposity. The less educated a person is, the greater the skill that is needed to communicate with him because the greater the possibility of misconstruction. The following conversation took place between a visitor and a grave digger on a Scottish island:

> *Visitor*:   It's very quiet round here.
> *Gravedigger*: Not so quiet as they there, sir.
> *Visitor*:   Yes, but I don't suppose people die round here often do they?
> *Gravedigger*: Only once, sir.
> *Visitor*:   Have you lived here all your life?
> *Gravedigger*: Not yet, sir!

On second thoughts, perhaps it was not the gravedigger who had the lesser intellect!

On the other hand, the higher a person's education, the more likely that there will be an emotional factor in the communication. To be meaningful, communication must take place in an atmosphere where perception is not clouded by fear, suspicion and grievance, and where a degree of trust has already been created. We all

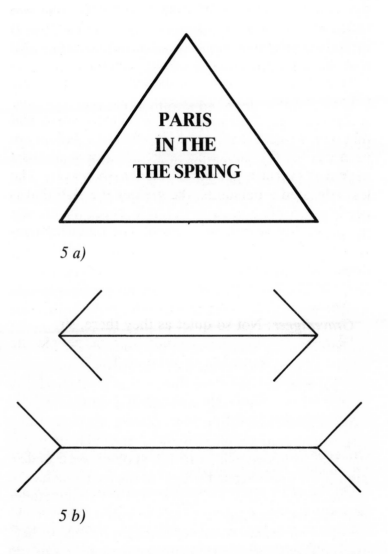

5 a)

5 b)

tend to hear what we want or expect to hear and to accept things within the context of our own experience. The two lines in Illustration 5(b) are in fact the same length but appear to be different because of the context in which each is placed. The message in Illustration 5(a) is, for most people, what they expect to hear rather than what is written.

We can all be deceived into thinking that the statement 'I see' from the person we are addressing means that he has actually understood. Of course, individuals can be helped by a training in writing and in effective speaking, but the safe way is to ensure that those who have information to impart should give deep thought to the people to whom they are trying to impart it, the queries that will arise in the listeners' minds and the language that will translate the message.

The question of language is important, yet it is not only the choice of words in written communication which also is vital, but the decision as to whether the communication should be written at all. The merits of oral or written communication are discussed in detail in a later section. However, there is seldom a substitute for face-to-face communication if that is practical, but as this can be done only with small groups of people extra time will be required to convey a message to a large number of people. Face-to-face contact makes it possible to get reactions to the spoken word and to modify the approach in the light of the changing face of the audience. In this connection, it is well to remember that the face and gestures of the communicator are equally important. Words of love from a face of hate are unlikely to impress! Written communications, on the other hand, though they cannot be tailor-made, have the advantages of speed, consistency and acting as a record. There is a place for both and the advantages of both must be weighed.

One study that can be put into practice is to offer the same problem to three different groups in three different ways. The first way takes the form of a simple presentation to individuals and the second involves a similar presentation to a group. In the third way, only a brief summary of the problem is presented to a group who are then invited to discuss it, so that a greater part of the information is brought to light only by the group involving themselves personally with the problem and asking questions about it.

A subsequent examination of the extent to which the three groups retain the information will normally show that the third method, with its two-way flow of information and active involvement by the audience, is very much more effective.

And the failures? Apart from the wrong choice of language, a communication can fail because it has not been thoroughly prepared, the reception has not been checked and the message has, in consequence, been ambiguous and unsystematic. The logical pattern used in presenting the message step-by-step is not acquired without practice. One other cause for failure remains to be listed, and that is the failure of the communicator to listen. Talking alone is not communicating as any attender at an average cocktail party will know.

11. The 'where' of communications

The 'where' or setting of the communication is important and is a major contributor to the atmosphere which will make that communication effective or otherwise. The choice is as wide as the variety of the message. It will range from a public meeting of a department to a formal interview between two people or an informal meeting outside company premises. Much will depend on how official the communication is to be.

When the message is a general one for a number of people and concerning, for example, an announcement of some new product or employee benefit, the conference room is the obvious choice. If discussion is to follow, people will be encouraged to join in if the chairs are arranged in a semicircle round the speaker so that he is not remote from his audience. The atmosphere of 'them and us' is easily fostered; it is not so easily overcome.

This applies to behaviour in the office as well. For how many visitors will a manager come round to the other side of his desk and sit down with his guest? Not doing so, certainly in some Government departments, tends to be regarded as a symbol of rank. You come round to sit with someone of equal or greater seniority, otherwise the barrier remains! The guideline should be a simple one. If the conversation is to take any length of time and is to be a friendly one it is a pity to have a desk between. On the other hand, if a rebuke is to be administered, however quiet the tone of voice, then the manager should remain on his side of the desk. Perhaps the other guideline should be that, if one is treating each individual with respect, then everyone, however junior, should be treated the same way.

Often it will be wise, if a manager feels there is some personal problem to be sorted out – if, for example, he feels that some home problem is affecting an employee's work and behaviour – to arrange an opportunity to meet and talk outside the office. In this way barriers will be broken down as much as possible and a subordinate will feel more inclined to speak freely and informally.

One means of communicating should be emphasised even though, alone, it is inadequate. It is just walking round a department or shop floor, chatting, getting the 'feel' of things. In a sense, this is almost a matter of courtesy. To take time to talk about inessentials is to recognise that if we are to spend eight hours or more each day with someone, then the relationship may as well be friendly! It is extraordinary how many managers either feel they have not time for this or, worse, that in some strange way they lose face by letting down their hair!

How many managers arrive in their office and stay, closeted in meetings or tied to the telephone, until they leave? Conversely, how many deliberately take time off to walk around their department? How many directors, when visiting other parts of the company deliberately build in time in their programme for this purpose? The habit of dividing life into compartments does not

make for good communications. The manager who
claims that his door is ever open may believe what he

The open door?

says, but no one is likely to feel they can pop in unless
the manager sometimes pops out to talk to them.

This aspect of 'where' has been stressed because so
much of the choice in the earlier paragraphs follows
basic and obvious rules. The creation of an atmosphere
of trust and open communication is likewise basic and
obvious, but less practiced. A very busy manager, General Eisenhower, had this to say on the subject:

At times I received advice from friends, urging me to give up or curtail visits to troops. They correctly stated that, as far as the mass of men was concerned, I could never speak personally to more than a tiny percentage. They argued, therefore, that I was merely wearing myself out, without accomplishing anything significant, so far as the whole Army was concerned. With this I did not agree. In the first place I felt that through constant talking to enlisted men I gained accurate impressions of their state of mind. I talked to them about anything and everything; a favourite question of mine was to enquire whether the particular squad or platoon had figured out any new trick or gadget for use in infantry fighting. I would talk about anything so long as I could get the soldier to talk to me in return.

I knew, of course, that news of a visit with even a few men in a division would soon spread throughout the unit. This I felt, would encourage men to talk to their superiors, and this habit I believe promotes efficiency. There is, among the mass of individuals who carry the rifles in war, a great amount of ingenuity and initiative. If men can naturally and without restraint talk to their officers, the products of their resourcefulness becomes available to all. Moreover, out of the habit grows mutual confidence, a feeling of partnership that is the essence of 'esprit de corps'. An army fearful of its officers is never as good as one that trusts and confides in its leaders.

'Chatting up people' is not necessarily communication but it does help to provide the atmosphere where communication can take place. A final coment on 'where'. The person who meets you by chance in the lift or in the passage and says, 'Oh, I've been meaning to get in touch with you to talk about . . .', invites the comment 'well, why didn't you?' and the feeling that what he had to say was not worth saying anyhow!

12. The 'who' of communications

We now come to the last of our serving men, 'who'. These servants are always on duty together and each must perform his task. Who should be told and who should be telling? Both questions must be asked.

A passenger transport company changed all the route numbers on the bus stops in its main station. Because there was no proper communication link the one group who were not informed of these changes were the drivers!

The question about who should be told has already been touched on in the 'what' of communications. Here it was seen that one should communicate as much rather than as little as possible, not only because there was a need to know the actual content of the message but also because there was a need to build up a climate of trust and openness.

In the same way, the objective of telling as many people as possible what is going on has the effect that even the most junior employee will work more efficiently if he is 'in the know' and made to feel a participant in the business of the company. Of course, this does not mean giving everyone complicated accounts which may be well above their need. It does mean, however, inculcating the *feeling* in each individual that he is party to what is going on and can ask more if he wants. This feeling is nourished even more by the manager taking time to talk and explain than by what he actually says.

It is also important to recognise that all employees will be far better ambassadors, both in letter and spirit, for the company in which they work if they, in turn, are able to communicate an understanding to the outside world. It was Tallyerand who said, 'Give me good internal policies and I will give you a good foreign policy.'

The opinion poll quoted earlier showed that the manager was the source from which people expected to hear all news. The figures showed that they often failed to get it in this way. The answer to the questions, 'who should tell?' is, normally, the manager, but there are frequently lapses from this ideal. A case came recently to my notice of a factory manager in a chemical company that was undergoing reorganisation. In walking into his manager's office to discuss a future engagement, he was told by that manager's secretary that arrangements had been made for him to be posted to another part of the country. At the best this was incompetence; at the worst it was weakness on the part of the boss. In either case it was disastrous and the factory manager handed in his notice.

The first rule is that if the news is bad or likely to build resistence, it is the job of the manager to face the employee. It is at such times that he will have to draw on the capital of goodwill and trust that he has been able to build up. The manager should *never* hide behind the words 'they have decreed', or 'it is company policy'. A manager, once he has earned that position, is identified with 'them'. He is the upholder as well as the transmitter of company policy. If he shows a lack of loyalty himself, he will certainly lose respect and invite the same attitude from others towards himself. Certainly, if the result of some policy is to disclose inequities that had not been anticipated, the manager will have a duty to see the matter is examined. He is a two-way communicater. But he is not a subverter!

One of the hardest things to communicate in a considered way is the message that someone is not up to standard. Of course it is easy to do this in a heated moment but that will invite an equally heated reply. The easy way is to leave the job to another, to continue to accept a second-class standard or to move an individual sideways. The notice that President Truman had on his desk, 'The buck stops here' should be the managers' guide and the test of his moral courage.

One aspect of 'who' which is demanding attention at present is that under the general heading of disclosure of information. Again, this book is aimed at the needs of the line manager and so the intricacies of parliamentary legislation are left aside. The essence of disclosure is surely that any business has a number of 'stakeholders' – people or groups who have an interest in its fortunes. Four major and generally accepted groups are the employees, shareholders, customers and the community. Only one of these groups is covered in any detail by legal requirements. The legal demands are likely to extend to others before long. The spirit, if not yet the letter, of the situation is that a business is accountable to each of its stakeholders and therefore each of them must be told the way in which the firm's responsibility to them has been discharged.

Summary

So much for the six serving men. Obvious? Perhaps so. Perhaps these points are all part of the management 'touch' – that instinct that the good manager has which makes him sensitive to the requirements of each situation. And yet, whatever instinct may be there, either circumstances or lack of conscious training seem frequently to lead to failure. And when they do, how often can this failure be attributed to not heeding one of these six questions? Each manager can ask how often *he* has not been put in the picture because *his* manager has not told him what is going on. And then he can ask how often has he been responsible for the experience with others?

There are two short items to be discussed before closing this section. The first is that we should not forget that silence is a potent communicator. A man walked into a room where two others were reading their newspaper. They continued to do so and after a time of shuffling, clearing his throat and generally drawing attention to his presence, the man walked out. One of the two men in the room then remarked to the other, 'Weren't we a little rude to that man?' 'Nonsense,' replied the second, 'we didn't say anything!' Likewise, the man who asks for a rise and is greeted by a stony silence gets the message all right.

The second matter in the measurement of communication is a negative measurement in that no one has walked out as a result of what a manager has said or done. It is harder to ensure effectiveness in a positive way. Nevertheless, there should be a check after the event to see that our words, spoken or written, have been understood and have covered all the questions that may have come into people's minds. This check is all too uncommon. Could it be that we are nervous of what we might find?

Case Study

The following case study is suggested for use in a communications training session. It should follow a session in which Kipling's serving men are discussed in some detail. Students should only have the first part of this study, and the answers to questions, which are suggested in the notes, should be drawn out by the students, with the instructor providing the details suggested in the notes, or any other variations he may wish.

The International Biscuit Manufacturers, adhering to Government Location of Industry Policy, have decided to move their London headquarters to a rural location near Oxford. The move, which will start in fifteen months' time, will be phased over a period of six months. Negotiations with a Mr Green in the local council have indicated that there will be full co-operation from the local authorities in matters of housing, schools, etc. The immediate problem is that the subject, until now confidential between the company and Mr Green's staff, is due to be discussed at an open meeting in a fortnight's time. An announcement to the company's staff, who are already aware that some move is in the air, is therefore desirable. The following should be considered when putting over the information:

(a)   What further information do you wish to ask the person who is setting this case study? (People will presumably need to know the numbers, sex, marital status, the job categories of the staff, and other London area locations.)

(b)   What questions would you want to ask Mr Green? (Questions can be expected here concerning schools, shopping areas, transport, priorities on housing, location details etc.)

(c)   What are your proposals, as the manager in charge of communications, for communicating this plan to company employees? (Plans should consider the use of Kipling's serving men and the various communications media. They should include press as well as internal announcements, and also arrangements that might be made for families of employees, and relocating those who do not wish to move.)

Check list for communications

What?   Do I tell the maximum or minimum?

   Am I being honest?

   Can I beat the grapevine?

Does my message relate to the recipient?

Does the recipient understand what I have said?

Why? Why is this message being passed?

Have I explained 'why' in simple language?

Have I given the opportunity to ask 'why'?

When? What is the correct time of the day/week for this message?

To what groups and in what order must it be passed?

Have I considered who gets the news first – employees or outsiders?

Is my message to different audiences synchronised?

In whose time is the communication made?

How? What language?

Written or spoken?

What demeanour?

Repetition of message?

Where? What sort of message is it?

Where is the appropriate place?

Does the employee pop in or do I pop out?

What about walkabout?

Who? Who tells?

Who should be told?

On whose side am I when communicating?

Does the buck stop here?

PART IV

The techniques of communications

Foreword

In the third section we discussed the use of Kipling's serving men in communication. We now look at some of the media and the choice of techniques that is open.

We should remind ourselves that there are four different ways in which communications can occur. The three most obvious and accepted methods are written, oral and visual. The fourth, less often considered and already mentioned in this book, is silence. The fact it is not considered does not mean it is infrequently used.

A number of different techniques can be used to communicate and, while there will certainly be specialists who can prepare professional presentations and translate messages into a variety of media, the line manager must be conversant in broad terms with their possibilities as well as their limitations.

13 Written communications

The employee newspaper

The merits or otherwise of newspapers, monthly magazines or house journals continue to be debated and the attempt to combine what are, in fact, distinct roles continues to be made.

A starting point, but one that is frequently overlooked, is that there cannot be any such thing as a monthly newspaper. A publication is a newspaper or it is something else; that is, it deals with news or it is concerned with history or some other matter. When an organisation produces a monthly publication in newspaper format, it is generally because they expect it to be more readable. An employee newspaper is a newspaper in every sense and the minimum frequency with which a genuine newspaper can be produced is probably weekly. Its objectives are threefold.

First, it will keep employees informed about company policies, practices and regulations, and about management objectives, plans, problems, successes and failures. There will almost certainly be a gap, when the objective is phrased like this, between what the manager wants to say and what his audience wants to hear. The editor has the task of presenting policies as news and translating regulations into headlines. Even then, only certain policies and regulations will be suited to this medium. Second, a newspaper will give the employees an understanding of the work they are doing, the products they are making and the reasons for the demands made on them in their jobs. Again, the editor will present information of this nature as news rather than regulations. Third, the paper will give employees news of themselves and their activities so that they feel more at home in their organisation. Such items start off by being news; they are easy to present and the main danger is the editor who confines the opportunity he has to reporting about the social trivia of the company club.

The newspaper has a number of advantages over other media. It can be personal and friendly, it is up to date and so a vehicle for fresh news, it is usually credible and, with wise handling, is less likely to be regarded as a propaganda vehicle. Much will depend on the stature, and thus the status of the editor himself. He must have access to top management and they, in turn, must feel it worth their while to spend time with him.

Finally a policy decision must be taken, which must be clearly understood by the editor, about the degree of independence that the editor should enjoy since, in the final analysis, such a publication, if not overtly a management tool is at least required to conform broadly with company policies. The company is paying for it; the sum allotted is, hopefully, the result of management decision but there should be other channels within the organisation for bringing pressure to pursue policies and practices that are different to those currently in force.

The house journal

Part of the reason for the dispute when choosing between a newspaper and a monthly journal is that, in a company where the readership will include a range of job interest, intellectual ability and geographical association, the inevitable result of a newspaper is that it will tend to cater for the lower end of the intellectual spectrum. A journal, on the other hand, by treating matters in greater depth, may find its appeal restricted to the other end. The attempt to combine something that satisfies both ends can be a success though often it is not.

House journals are produced monthly, quarterly or at even less frequent intervals. They tend to suffer because few companies are willing to devote sufficient resources, both financial and editorial, to enable them to compete successfully with the enormous number of commercial and other magazines available from the news-stands, some of which are always to be found in an employee's home. The result is that house journals are often unread.

The advantages of such a magazine, if well produced, are that it does allow the treatment of a subject in greater depth and thus in a less ephemeral manner than a paper. If it is a prestige publication, it will find its way outside the company and will be displayed in employee's homes. Its life may be extensive.

A policy decision, both with the journal and the paper, has to rule on whether a price is charged. On the one hand, it is true that paying for something tends to make one appreciate it. On the other, the bother of collecting the money, (which is anyhow unlikely to be the real cost of production) and the likelihood that a number of employees may decline to purchase the publication even at a nominal cost, may work against charging anything at all. In brief, the house journal is valuable if it is used to reinforce a newspaper but probably should not stand alone as the only employee publication available.

The employee bulletin

A bulletin is a message on paper distributed to a large or small number of people. It can be produced and circulated quickly though, being less formal, it should usually be reinforced by one or more of the other techniques. A point to remember is that anything which gives the impression of being amateur will militate against the acceptance of a high standard in other spheres of company activity. This applies to the use of all media.

Notice-boards

One of the oldest and cheapest means of communication available is the notice-board. It is also one of the most misused. Notice-boards are frequently just a mortuary in which stale announcements slowly pile-up. A notice-board announcement should rarely be used by itself as a means of communication. However, it can lend emphasis and repetition to items which have been or will be, covered in greater depth through other media. The following criteria should apply to the use of notice-boards if they are to be in any way effective.

1. They should be properly designed as should the notices placed on them.
2. They should be reserved for notices that have been initiated by the manager in charge of internal communication.
3. Permanent, statutory notices should be kept separate from communications notices.
4. Social club or other notices should likewise be confined to a separate board.
5. Different coloured or type designs should signify different kinds of announcement (e.g. appointments, press cuttings, personnel etc.)
6. Boards should be prominently displayed.
7. The date of posting and removal should be included and shown on each notice so that employees can always expect to find fresh information.
8. A responsible person in each location should see to the posting and removal of notices.

Letters to employees at home

This is an effective but potentially dangerous medium and therefore one to be used sparingly. It will normally be used only by the senior executive who writes a personal letter direct to the employee at home. There is a tight-rope to be trodden here, between the effectiveness of the method and the invasion of the Englishman's castle. It can be trodden. Another danger is that if this method of communication is only used at times of crises, the letter becomes associated with drama. A more acceptable policy is that these letters, though infrequent, are regular and deal with matters which, if not critical, are nevertheless of company-wide impor-

The letter at home

tance. Given the dangers, there is still much to be said for this means of communication since it is read in the relaxed atmosphere of the home. Implicit in its use is that the subject matter is for home discussion. It is a useful method of dealing with situations where rumour or the grapevine may be the only alternative sources of information or where family, as opposed to just employee, welfare is at stake.

Enclosures in pay-slips?

The answer is no! Administratively, there may be a temptation to enclose information which does not relate to an employee's pay within his pay-slip because it is a sure way of reaching him. A pay-slip should be sacrosanct and, of all potential invasions, this is the worst!

Summary on written communications

Advantages: They are prepared, can be checked for accuracy and signed off.

Dissemination can be quick, widespread, consistent and synchronised.

A record is kept.

Disadvantages: Feedback takes time.

The message cannot be altered in the light of reactions so it is mainly one-way communication.

It is impersonal.

14. Oral communications

Oral, as opposed to written, communications likewise have their advantages and disadvantages. They are useful because they allow the communicator to gauge the reaction of his audience. They can be tailor-made for each type of audience and feed-back is immediate. On the other hand if no record is kept this can lead to misrepresentation. Oral communications also take time since they are less effective as the audience gets larger and, ideally, manageable groups of people need to be given the message at any one time. Finally the consistency of written communications is missing if the same message has to be given to several groups by different speakers. As a general rule oral communications will need to be backed up by the written word. This will allow the speed and universality of the written communication to balance the slowness but intimacy of the spoken word.

Meetings

Meetings tend to be unpopular with managers who question the time taken by people from their work. By now, no reader should be taken in by this argument since communicating is part of the job and should take place in job hours. It is as important for employees to know what is going on as it is for more senior people to attend courses lasting days or weeks. Both interruptions from normal routine are necessary.

Meetings can include many degrees from the formal to the informal. Whatever the degree of formality, certain rules apply. The meeting must be structured. This means that the person calling it has done his homework: he knows why he has called it, what he wants to say and what he needs to achieve. He has a clear idea of who should take part and he will check that they are there. He will order his presentation and ensure that, even with questions, he retains control. He will take care about the setting so that attention is not diverted by discomfort or other distractions. Finally, he will see that a record of the meeting is kept and he will check later to see that its purpose has been achieved. In short, he will use Kipling's servants at meetings as he will for any other communication.

Instruction

Although much has been said on the subject of instruction, the basic rules are simple. The pupil will reflect the capacity of the teacher to be logical and to enthuse, so first of all the pupil must be motivated to learn. Dante spoke of the ingredients of 'awe and curiosity' in the learning process. Given this basis, the instructor must then prepare his subject so that it is presented in a logical sequence with all irrelevancies discarded. It must be taught in simple, manageable steps with an opportunity for checking receptivity at each stage.

Then what has been taught must stand the test of practice. One more admonition and that is that the instructor should not presume he can instruct, but should subject himself to the criticism of his peers and colleagues before he ventures his skills on his pupils.

Interviews

An interview between two individuals may have been called by either one of them. In either case it will have an objective and, in the course of meeting this, attitudes may have to be modified. An interview can have a variety of purposes: to seek a job, to resolve a difference of opinion, to agree a proposed course of action, to register a complaint and so on. The spectrum of atmosphere will range from discussion to conflict. The manager may have requested the interview or not but, at the end, certain facts and opinions will have been reviewed and a decision hopefully reached.

As much as ever, the 'serving men' are all important in the interview. First, in providing the setting that meets the particular needs of the case; second, in handling the interview in a way that removes any inhibitions caused by rank, emotion, prejudice etc.; third, in following up the interview to see that its purpose has been achieved and its decisions recorded.

Again, a final comment to a subject that is only sketched here. The initiative is with the person who calls the interview. There may be occasions when the other person wishes to seize this initiative. If this is allowed to happen, the interview generally begins to go wrong.

Radio and Tannoy

It has been said that Music While You Work is the antidote to Pay as You Earn. Too many plants – and indeed offices – suffer from an intrusion of loudspeakers which, when they are not being used for announcements, send out musical and other programmes. In fact, there have been some excellent experiments where people in repetitive and boring jobs can listen in to music, news summaries, educational programmes, language training and so on. The difference is that they have private head-sets! As a call system, the pocket radio carried by many supervisers is effective and unobtrusive. As an announcement system in a large concern, tannoy may be useful but should be used sparingly. Silence, which we know can be a powerful communicator, was once described as a state which existed in Heaven for half an hour.

Taking notes

When the purpose of oral communication is to convey information, it is important to see that it is conveyed! The well-known 'whispering exercise' in the Army involved passing a whispered sentence down a line of people. The classic conversion of meaning occured during World War I when the message 'Send reinforcements, I'm going to advance,' was heard as 'Lend three and fourpence, I'm going to a dance.' The safeguard is to insist that, when the information is in turn going to be passed on by others, notes are taken.

None of the above paragraphs attempts to be exhaustive. There are many media. The essential is that the manager, in preparing his message, must also think about how he is going to put it across. He must weigh the advantages and disadvantages of using one or more of the different techniques and he must insist that the professionalism with which they are used is of a high standard. Above all, he must be sure that he knows what he has to say. To open his mouth before an audience will not alone guarantee that anything worth hearing will emerge.

15. Visual communications

Visual techniques for communication may stand alone; often they will be used in conjunction with some other technique. The manager wants to know what is available as well as some of the pitfalls he may encounter.

Films, film strips, slides and cassettes

Apart from their use in training sessions all of the above can supplement other forms of communication.

The first consideration about films is that they are expensive. They can be instructive and educational and they take time to prepare, so they will be produced to meet a recurring need or a long-standing issue rather than a means for quick response to any fast moving situation. That they cannot easily be altered is another reason why the message has to be more than ephemeral. However, films bring prestige to a firm and instil pride in its employees so for this reason many people will want their say, and unless final authority is clearly delineated, the result of compromise and committees may be a camel!

Film strips are cheap and quick to produce though they, too, cannot be easily altered. They are excellent

'Filmstrips are easy to produce'

for instruction and the equipment they need for showing in a large number of locations is simple and inexpensive. For most purposes, however, they can be replaced by equally effective slide presentations.

Slide presentations are also very simple to use. Their great merit is that they can be amended and frames substituted in the light of a changing situation, while their quality is just as good as that of film strips. As in the case of any media, the fact that its preparation is simple and inexpensive does not, however, mean it can afford to be amateurish.

Video-cassettes, plugged in to a standard television set are becoming increasingly popular as a way of presenting a message to a dispersed population. They are more expensive than filmstrips or slides and so will tend to be used for prestige purposes such as an annual statement by the chairman, an explanation of some company policy or an announcement of an important product.

All the above techniques pre-suppose that there is standard equipment throughout an organisation. When the intention is to use these techniques outside the organisation, it is wise to presume that the necessary plugs, screen, wiring and other conditions for their use are either missing or untested despite assurances to the contrary, so that everything must be tested by the user himself. He may then come to the decision to use no techniques at all!

Remote conference facilities

Modern communications will make the moving of bodies from one location to another as out-of-date as bartering cattle. There are better uses of management time than travelling. Indeed, the vogue phrase in America is 'Live where you please, travel for pleasure, communicate to work'. Much of the equipment for allowing the executive to work from home is available, though its use is still inhibited by inadequate postal facilities.

Remote conference facilities and closed circuit television are of course with us now. They are not techniques that only large organisations can handle, although they tend to be more expensive than some. It is, however, important to remember that when public transmission lines are used, lead time is required.

Visual communications such as these have an important part to play but they are naturally one-way communication techniques and so do not allow for reactions
and feed-back. When they are used for company meetings, therefore, it is as well for the meetings to be conducted by a manager who has himself been personally
briefed and who will elicit audience response.

16. Silent communications

17. Technology and communication

A factor that inevitably greatly influences the study of communications is that this is an age of accelerated change characterised by a variety of technical advances. The purpose of this brief chapter is to remind managers of the backcloth to their operations and to indicate some of the points they have to consider in their work.

Time and space

When communications were confined to physical transport (or even smoke signals!) scales of time and distance were imposed on the sending and reception of messages. To illustrate the time-scale, in 1834 an urgent message told Sir Robert Peel in Rome to return to London because he had been made Prime Minister; the journey took him thirty-two days to arrive. As an illustration of the distance scale, the last City state in Europe disappeared only in 1872. The limitations of communications forgave people for thinking small and slow.

Today, communications are released from these physical limitations. Computer networks, for example, allow full and instant dissemination of information across the country, continent or even the globe. Other facilities, not least television, weld together outlying parts of an organisation, conveying without pity every inflexion of insincerity and exposing mercilessly every tendency to pontificate. And, of course, words spoken in a hall in London can be heard as quickly in Australia as at the back of the room.

Speed and distance

The speed of modern communications reduces turn-around and reaction time. Whether the news is carried by the accepted media or the grapevine, it gets there quicker. The implication for managers is that they must, in preparing their communication, take into account the speed at which the process they start will continue. They must also, at the same time, prepare for the 'second round', in that they must include in their original thinking, not only the preparation of the communication itself, but the likely reaction to it.

The complication of a different time system with global communications is touched on elsewhere. Anyone who works for an international organisation will know the way in which news can percolate unofficially between nightfall on one side of the Atlantic and dawn on the other.

Impersonalisation

'Things behave: people experience', says Laing. Hence the emphasis, in a technological age, on human skills.

At a time when, from the employee's point of view, the intimate details of pay, benefits, allowances and personnel records can be held in computer files from which, to the observer, mistakes emerge with an almost human frequency, the conviction that a manager is still personally interested in an individual is vital. It may be sometimes that a degree of inefficiency is preferable to a lapse of humanity.

The immediate and general availability of information can, in theory, constitute a threat to some of the middle echelons of management. Moreover, the availability of the same information at head office or peripheral level constitutes a temptation to centralise control. Information is power! Both the threat and the temptation in some instances, particularly in the United States, have been realised. Both should be resisted. The removal of levels of management may be an offshoot of an information society in which the hierarchical concept of management becomes less meaningful. On the other hand, the emphasis on the communications content of a manager's job is more important as techniques multiply. The centralisation of information and control is also unwise. In fact, with the existing techniques for dissemination, it is possible to upgrade the quality of decision-making and responsibility entrusted to a subordinate simply because he will have the information to do the job. And, with the new information networks, it is easier to carry out a post-factum audit of a subordinate's actions, so he will be less able to talk his way out of situations by virtue of his charm and personality!

The information explosion

Finally, one effect of technology has been the information explosion. Information which, by one definition or another, received its first doubling in the year 1750, is now doubling once every four years. To sift this, to keep pace with it, to pass on what is relevant, is no easy task. Computer systems help, but all managers must realise that this process looks like continuing and we are moving fast into an area where the information business is becoming the major industry of our times.

In summary, let it be said once more that techniques should be on tap, not on top. Technical advances can aid management; they can also cause problems. In no case can they screen or substitute for management. The human consequences of technical change can be painful or not according to the way we handle them. Were the Luddites, who broke up machines, really resisting progress, or were they reacting to the fact that they had just not been told what was going on or helped to adjust to change?

Management, now of all times, has to be in a position to understand change and then to inform and lead those affected by it.

Summary

Techniques help communication; they are not a substitute for it. Emerson once said to someone, 'What you are is shouting so loud that I cannot hear what you say.' If the technique and the real message that is coming through are not consistent, then it is better to have no technique at all. Techniques can underline any insincerity. They cannot bluff.

Only when the message is thought out carefully and is sincere can the technique then be used to enhance it and help the receptivity and understanding of the audience. In an educated work force, consmetics are definitely going out of fashion.

We have to remember that the techniques described in this chapter are mass methods of communication. The common denominator is, therefore, going to be relatively small. A mass communication contains only a portion that is relevant to everyone who receives a message. The passing of the message does not guarantee that it is received. This is why stress has to be laid continually on the *understanding* that is conveyed, whatever the means used.

Index

115